LOPLOP in a red CITY

Also by Kenneth Pobo

Booking Rooms in the Kuiper Belt
Bend of Quiet
Glass Garden
Introductions
Ordering: A Season in My Garden
Musings from the Porchlit Sea

Chapbooks

Highway Rain / When The Light Turns Green
Placemats / Save My Place
Ice And Gaywings / Tiny Torn Maps
Contralto Crows / Closer Walks / Tea on Burning Glass
Fitting Parts / Trina and the Sky / Something To Be Said
Crazy Cakes / Postcards from America
Kenneth Pobo's Greatest Hits / Open To All
Cicadas and Apple Trees / A Barbaric Yawp on the Rocks
Ravens and Bad Bananas / Yes: Irises
Ferns On Fire / A Pause Inside Dusk
Evergreen / Billions of Lit Cigarettes

LOPLOP in a red CITY

Kenneth Pobo

POEMS

CIRCLING RIVERS

RICHMOND, VIRGINIA

CIRCLING RIVERS

PO Box 8291
Richmond, VA 23226

www.circlingrivers.com

Cover image: *Loplop Introduces Himself,* by Max Ernst. Private collection

ISBN: 978-1-939530-03-5

Visit CirclingRivers.com to subscribe to news of our authors and books, including book giveaways. We never share or sell our list.

for Stan

Contents

Crow at Daybreak

Empire of Lights

Painting by René Magritte

Inside the house our peace rumbles.
Mom and dad haunt opposite ends of the couch.
Did I mention they're dead?

It doesn't matter. I'm not living either.
I go to school, play guitar, watch TV,
and argue with my sister Ag who doesn't

argue back. The house, a still cat. Gunfire
breaks the calm, like cathedral
bells, mournful, lasting. I'm used to blue sky

and clouds even at night. I dream in
the day but have none when I fall asleep.
No one in this family dreams at night.

Dawn-chirping birds, we're hungry,
flying off, then grabbing a branch
to watch time's red bear raise his paw

and knock over the mailbox. Someday
we might decide to come alive. Porchlights
will shine either way. Someone may move away,

perhaps me. For now the maple that hides
my window wants company—who am I
to deny that wish?

Interior with Seated Couple

Painting by Marianne von Werefkin

She wishes he'd lodge himself
in a lit wick. He would,
but fears another night
of pall bearers carrying
his own body across his brain's

twisting streets. She pictures herself
on a train, no destination, countryside
pop-up storms, hay wagons,
armless scarecrows. Afraid
to travel with or without him or anyone,
she won't go.

A clown, silence tries to make them laugh,
falls dead at their feet.

Composition with Glove

Relief Sculpture by Pablo Picasso

About my birth, the stories
change. My mother is dead.
I try to remember what she said
about my arrival. It's dust. Mostly.
A Caesarean, I had hair

the nurses combed. In my fifties now,
dust feels closer.

The email arrives about a friend
my age with prostate cancer.

Carl Sagan: *At our deaths*
the light we see may be that of
our entrance into the world.
Light and dust—juggling,
one tries to get the upper hand.

Picasso: *Art washes the soul*
of the dust of the everyday. Memory
covers over with a fine silt. Soon
we can't blow it away. We find
strange patterns, trace lines
that disappear, become something

unrecognizable. Even my body
looks like dust when lines

form, the hand that surely
can't be mine but is

grabbing at a darkness turning
to bright flecks that fall and fade.

Mystery and Melancholy of a Street

For decades I've been the little girl
rolling her hoop down a strange street,
a shadow creeping up. I have a name
for it, Death. Maybe it will overlook me

a while longer or until the hoop gets away
and lands against a fading arcade. What if
I've misnamed the shadow? It could be
Life—I want it to stop and talk to me,

let me rest from rolling the hoop,
but Life may have many streets to walk on,
people with a stronger need to talk.
I could hide in the circus wagon, wait

and see who the shadow is, but I'm scared
of the dark, scared I'll get trapped
and be taken far off. I grew up in
a land with purple lilacs and salmon iris.

I didn't want to leave but I did. I remember
Nature as the aunt I loved who moved away
and died. It may be dusty doorways
and nervous buildings from now on. The shadow,

who knows, could be my own,
some form of me that dissolves
in motion.

Daybreak

Collage by Emmy Bridgwater

In our dark house, we barely see
dried rain spots on the glass. A favorite
poem says they've all gone into the world

of light. But we are here.
Maybe mom rests between
the Meyer Lemon and the princess flower.

Light connects all things, doesn't it?
Even darkness. Time to turn off our day,
make a space for dreams to thicken

like hoya leaves.

Hubbub

"I fear hubbub" — Emmy Bridgwater

In our kitchen you think you're opening
a jar of your mother's tomato soup.

A hairy Pandora, this is
your moment to release a hubbub.

We argue until silence brings in the paper
it reads while sniffing burnt toast.
Conversation drops out
of our mouths like teeth. Soon we
just make sounds. Words cut

our lips. Hubbub kicks over a pail
of dirty water. Peace clicks its tongue
but we don't let it in. The kitchen
sneaks off with the den. We're left

in the nowhere of middle looking out
at two distances that chafe.

Euclid's Last Stand

Painting by Penelope Rosemont

Broken prisms on the bay
window's sill.

Dogs of dust drop
on grouchy orchids. Birds think

grass is a big casino,
gamble with breeze chips.

Dour-faced, the owl
must have lost. My aunt Cass

looked dour too,
died a millionaire,

not in money, but in her thimble
collection. I stand still

while the earth flirts
with the sun who one day

will crush it in his hairy arms.
Ah, love! A faint smell of

pomegranates
before that fatal kiss.

The Hopes at Home (1973-1977)

Painting by Howard Hodgkin

Black tilts. Spills surround them,

a yard or a giant
wedding ring. A green
or white smudge dots
yellow moments,

flops onto red. At edges
of their lives it gets a touch

lighter. Deep center,
wild color—do they recognize it
or spend so much time in the dark
that color becomes

an impossible destination,
a dream they often have,
gone by morning, so they
hunt color, a promise

unfulfilled, a bungled Eden,
where lovers
somehow miss each other.

Portrait of a Woman Wearing a Biedermeier Dress

Painting by Gabriele Munter

A tight bodice. Perhaps
her soul, like the dog

that escaped from Mary,
Queen of Scots' dress

when she was executed,
may yet escape. Ever since

she was young, strong hands
held her down, made her

mouth disappear. Fathers
and mothers keeping watch

all the time. Now she wants
to play, even sing—

an empty prison, the dress
no longer cages her.

Dick and Betsy Smith

Painting by Howard Hodgkin

Planets near absolute zero
fascinate Dick. Betsy claims life
is a garden—any petal offers
a cool lake, has no interest
in planets. Dick scoffs, says Eden
made gardens passé. Both

sit in a scent
of melting candles.
Immaculate lamps,
stiff and formal,
plan a takeover.
Magazines keep alert.
Dick and Betsy
fall asleep, enter rooms

in each other's dreams, call
for each other as floors fail,
Ceilings burst, wake

without saying
where they were.

Vincent Van Gogh

1. Brussels

The journey began in gray
The first unsure strokes
prophesies sketched in seawater
Mysticism the scar
on every face
Never enough cash for paint
A need to create

a new form of halo
A chalk mark on time
The artist fills
with a million mouths
He isn't eating enough
Dreams break up like ice
He must section infinity
into parts of apple
One decade to plant and harvest
The taste is fatal
He will welcome it and despair
at once

We will never see a star
as a distant shore again

2. *The Hague*

It's true I'm sitting here lonely,
*   but … my work perhaps speaks to my*
*   friend, and whoever sees it will not*
*   suspect me of being heartless.*

A black pencil sketch   Sorrow
a woman
her hair clotting on her back
head shielded by an elbow
She follows us through wars
and a dropped bomb
Her lantern tears
light our highways
A temptress gone to seed
a victim
seen through haze in a mirror

Vincent feels empathy
Someone says "You are no artist"
The doorway empty
Back home talk
inspires talk   When will he
make some-
thing of himself

His silence too
sorrow

3. Nuenen

A woman pours coffee
to hungry potato eaters
Their plates steam with labor
Under one lamp
in each face he sees a cemetery
with rows of anonymous crosses

The easel in his room   a wound
turning skin to canvas

4. Paris

Simplicity
pink and white
tree branches
The sky drips
tallow from the sun
He works in Cormont's studio

The former evangelist hears
a wafer crack
searching Tanguy's face
A thatched self-portrait
a blue coat and a green hat

This is the minute
of seed angling into root
A city at his back
a shadow
between sputtering gaslamps

5. Arles

His face a vulture
over Gauguin's chair
Hills swarm at the window
Onions on a plate   a letter
an open wine bottle
He hopes the yellow house
will found a new Japan
Layer by layer
he paints over his mouth
and eyes

unhooks an ear
and mails it
Gauguin calls it quits
Japan stillborn
Still he accomplishes
the peach   sun
globes uneaten

6. St. Remy

For weeks he's painting in the field
a torn coat among weeds

For my own work
I'm risking my life
and half my mind is gone.
Within a year of his death
the hand
trembles

opening a grain of wheat
The center hurls toward the edge
Paint flung   a fierce candle
the ground swirling
new blood in each leaf
Sky   a rhythm
played to deaf ears
What he hears
draws his finger to the wick

The hand becomes the brush

Line surrenders to curve
Even the human figure
isn't safe

7. Auvers

Something flies across the brain
A shot heard in a cornfield
begins a journey
Earth tilts
He falls toward roots

Van Gogh's Crows

Crows took his body up to heaven—
a small room,
an easel, good bread on the table,

wine. A small flock got him there.
They flew back to earth—
black wings

perfect for mourning flapped
over a harvested wheat field, wind
dragged a sack of winter.

Odilon Redon's World

I stank at geometry—why
learn what makes
a triangle a triangle? My teacher said,

"It will make you logical."

Not logical, I flunked.
In fact, I'm a failure
except I know a good
zinnia when I see one.
That's not a small thing!

I know many people both logical and successful.
Some get involved in strange
triangles. What are they
trying to prove? Redon

could be right—you walk
through the world hunched over
from a huge gambling die

on your back. The forest
gives no direction, only
deeper shadows. Night

overcomes the edges, a dark
zinnia you see and smell
but can't prove its petals
give light.

The Greeting

Painting by Paul Delvaux

Sometimes you think
you're a businessman
in a brown suit walking
out of the house, expect
to trip on the tricycle, but find
you're in Pompeii,
don't sense the explosion

at hand. Your family often
volcanic—this morning
the door opens, a distant
volcano like the dad
who beat you up. You
greet a naked woman,
like she's the
garbage man. A bee

in your hat stings you
again and again. Time.
It buzzes, dies.
Much to do.
Move along.

In Chrustov's House Near St. Prex

Painting by Marianne von Werefkin

A single blossom sets a table
cloth on fire. When you sit alone
behind a plate, your life over
or seeming that way, the bouquet

says the river inside the heart
that can't be crossed stills
and allows passage. Dishes negotiate
the inch between us,

less than an inch apart,
with a floury smell. The tenuous lamp
knows your name
and secrets. Night thickens like batter.

In the morning you spread butter on,
forget all the arguments you had
about truths like firm
stems turning brown.

Rendezvous of the Friends

It's the usual thing—when friends
come over, they head for the kitchen.
I'm a poor cook, impatient. A slow
simmer makes me crabby. Tonight

is weird. My friends avoid the kitchen.
They've come to see a mountain
that bolted up out of the ground
like a spring coneflower. How it got there,
who knows? I wouldn't allow anything
to dwarf our forget-me-nots—
tiny blue flowers sing louder than
many a mountain, but they're hard

to see. My friends never climb mountains.
Most prefer swings and Lazy Boys. Indolence
takes our hats, puts them in a deep closet,
and we forget them. The mountain holds
moonlight on a leash. None of us
sings well, but we hum, hoping
to coax the mountain into a lovely pine
needle cha cha. If not,

we can return to the kitchen and talk
about the many ways our lives are going
badly. The many ways our lives are going.

Bust of a Man Asleep amid Flowers

Watercolor Painting by Odilon Redon

Before he falls asleep, he and his
sweetheart have tea. She's been angry
with him all day. When they reconcile,

kind of, he slips out to the prairie,
sits under the moon, having tea
with her sweetheart, while Saturn undresses.

The man hopes he won't dream,
sees himself as Pegasus, but no
winged creature ever visits at night.

Most of life is drab, like old linoleum—
tonight, again, no rescue comes,
but poppies, daisies, and roses sneak up,

open buds wide, shield him from sprites
that play practical jokes. In the morning
he tells his sweetheart he's forgotten

his dream. He walks to the cramped shop
in town which barely survives
year after year, shelves of glass

figurines he makes in the back room:
animals, flowers, and heroes that dream
about their maker, love and fear him.

Get Far Enough Out

Loplop Introduces Loplop

Painting by Max Ernst

I have a painting to show you.
It's the real me.

Or it was when I painted it. Now
I think someone else painted it,
a stranger. Does it matter
who signs what? Maybe while

painting, but later, once I, Loplop,
am flotsam, my name will drop
one more feather,

falling, blowing away. Even
in death my feathers will travel,
will enter the world in ways
I never could—

they will be my soul.

Loplop

Painting by Max Ernst

Half bird, half man,
something that resembles
both. This could easily be me.

As I escape
the ground, my parts
start to fall off. It's common—

the Scarecrow got scattered,
put back together, and still
ruled Oz. The body want a map

to return to the Earth
or, to get lift,
we have to let bits

of our selves go. How much
is it worth, to poke our heads
in the sky? What

must we surrender to float,
a hot air balloon,

not bird, not human,
not much of anything,
but free.

Loplop Introduces a Young Girl

Painting by Max Ernst

May I present to you the girl
who doesn't exist but does it so well
you assume she does. When

her frog croaks, Time leaps
from its mouth. She prefers birds
awking in treetop tiffs. After her birth,

a scarlet tanager carried her
to a swing set on top of the Earth
that scientists don't see.

Creaking swings disturb
mating integers. She grew up
to be brilliant and a practical joker. Ask

the lavender deer about that time
when she tricked him into swallowing
a whole water fall. She laughed so hard.

Hearing Death snapping oak branches,
she makes it tomato soup. She has
millennia left anyway, her scepter

made of sleeping hurricanes
like windy irons on a bed
that breathes and blooms.

Loplop Presents a Flower or Anthropomorphic Figure with Shell Flower

Painting by Max Ernst

A green bird could fly
away if you look at it funny

or it might stay. Either way
you keep moving

even if you stand still,
fleshrock. Your breath,

a highway spooling across
the countryside. Somebody

who took your milk money
in grade school pilots a plane—

you sit in 6E. He threatened
to kill you if you told. What's this

turbulence? You've felt it
ever since you were born,

bumps that may mean bupkis,
clouds taking attendance before

they disappear for good. You
barely see the bird—he's still

there, a still life,
heart beating,

a tiny beak
that can swallow you whole.

The Birth of the Idol

Painting by René Magritte

Land runs from water to
the comforts of lemon squares and tea
among Victorian houses. The mannequin

chooses between water's wild whips
and the land whose hornets hang
like pendants, wishes

undialed days would last,
has tried to give birth for centuries—
it's uncomfortable to wait that long,

so it follows the wind's hoofprints
back to Eden, still flowering, still
off limits, a closed park to sneak into.

The Giantess

Painting by Leonora Carrington

Don't think I'm not thinking because
my head is small. My body thinks too,
differently. Birds hatch from thoughts, fly
over my skin nest. Beneath me,

the yellow world thinks sad thoughts,
keeps running, it's less dangerous than
standing still. They wonder do I
mean to hurt them or if, being closer

to heaven, could I stuff a few prayers
in a god's ear so they don't have to enter
time's gray boat? They must enter.
I too must enter, but I won't fit—

I've never fit in, my strength
and grief. People worry one day
I will need to sit, and such a movement
would destroy the world or

their place in it. They don't know
that I become invisible, fall
asleep among them and they think I'm still
standing. A giantess, like a question mark,

should always be upright. I bring
down to them the question that I am,

I have no answers. To anything.
I don't need them. Or I need them

to create a new kind of fog,
one that invents a primary color,
washes it in a stream, lets it cover
the ground without ever lifting.

Epona, Goddess of the Herds

Painting by Maurice Denis

Women bring animals,
offer Epona prayers
which seep between rocks.
On her horse, Epona
offers no words.
Their concern for beasts
moves her: within a month
one recovers from
a bad illness, another
is with child. Still
the fertility and travel
goddess rests in
the forest's closing
eye. Autumn's red
hooks dig into trees—
Epona's calm
feeds deep roots.

Ophelia among the Flowers

Painting by Odilon Redon

To clarify the dreams of flowers,
an interpreter gets wounded,

a single hand hurt in the dark.
I gave up hope, knew that the rose

would offer secrets to me, a woman
carried away by a stiff current. Are you

losing hope too? Here, take this garland
I made when I learned the sun

warms only corpses. No forget-me-not
shies from a cemetery plot—

they bloom in the breath of who
you loved.

Morning breaks. Look—
an impossible garden overhead.

The Return of Ulysses

Painting by Giorgio de Chirico

When our living room gets cranky,
the Lazy Boy floats to the window.
The coffee table eats a crumb cake
I so gently laid down on it. Even the fireplace
throws snowballs at us. When strangers appear
I wish they were dead relatives and friends,
but they never come. Instead,

Ulysses drifts on a throw rug, blathers
about adventures. One time his little boat
had on board Penelope and Telemachus.
She had given up stitching and Tel preferred
dancing to battle. Ulysses
shrugs when we ask if it's fun being king.
The living room listens,
perhaps starstruck. When it's just us again,

we turn on the floor lamp—like seeing the sun
lean against the wall, yellow
lips forming a tentative O.

Sidhe, the White People of the Tuatha de Danaan

Painting by Leonora Carrington

As a kid, you envied the juggler.
Even now you hope
one of the balls tossed up by Danu,

a white bull and wonderful mother,
is a star that bolts from her chest—
she doesn't drop a single one.

You could stay all night,
but a juggler must move on
you've imposed long enough.
You leave a gift, songs
from blue delphiniums.

Triumphal Entry

Painting by James Ensor

Jesus appears in the sky
but another star's on trial
so no cameras cover his
return. We're in basements

inhaling money. He walks
unrecognized, wonders why
we've spent centuries building him
churches. Has it all come down

to fire sales, credit debt,
and investments? For this,
I should've stayed where
angels sing to 45s played

on cloud stereos, he thinks,
but since he's back anyway,
he decides to stop in at
Raffles, a nearby gay bar,

and visit friends who
buy him a drink
and invite him to judge
the Mr. Leatherman competition.

Kurt Schwitters

When critics say my art stinks,
I add them to my trash piles
and make a collage. They look
half alive. Hitler tried to drown

my fire. A phoenix, I rise from
refuse. The one leader I bow to—
the trash man, his truck
transporting glorious muck.

Franz Marc Painting before the War

Behind color and flesh,
something theologians
can't box up,
scholars can't hammer—

the soul he pokes
out of a color
makes a home on canvas—

he paints until war turns
his body into a red hole,
pokes his own soul
free from the skin.

Marionette Theatre—Jawlensky and Marianne von Werefkin in the Foreground

Painting by Marianne von Werefkin

Who or what holds strings over us,
lifts our arms, crashes
our bodies together?

We move as we must, enjoy
the dance we resent
doing. Maybe the

marionettes on stage enjoy theirs too—
they come alive, blood circulates,
ideas birth in wood chips.

My lover will be
famous, perhaps remembered
like Watteau. When he's dead,

no one will know what moved his hand
when he would have preferred
to rest. I can't say what moves

my own hand or why a dark
blue light can wound or delight me—
we keep trying to break

whatever holds us against
our will. Color a scissors
almost cutting us free.

El Sueno

Painting by Frida Kahlo

In my dream, animals drove people
around in buses made of mist.
We drove them around in silken word taxis.

Above the bed, several former selves met
in secret, argued, made threats.
After I woke, Tree said he saw me smiling:

"Hills built beneath your lids."
Hills? Opinionated rivers. Night,

my fourth grade teacher Miss Lana
told me, is like monkey bars.
Climb and climb but you'll never
touch Andromeda. How wrong she was!
Morning, an ant

on the bread board, bumps
against a crumb, a new day
stuck on each of his thirteen antennae.

The Dance on the Shore

Painting by Edvard Munch

After nailing ourselves to each other
we melt over artery tubes
The heart just not in it tonight
Blue shadows un-
       wind into fetuses
Breasts surge from a green carpet
We breathe in red hair of fog
Cannibals trade smiles
a scene our hunting fathers loved
    Rose floating
in a dish of colored stones
Lanterns twitch   snakes in mid-air
Wine glasses go up in alizarin crimson
We dance just outside the sun's orange
mouth opening slightly over a hedge
You hear a shriek I hear a shriek
Someone weird dissolves right before us
Space crammed with vegetation   Yellow
spirals jamming furiously   at nothing

Syssigy

Painting by Leonora Carrington

We're not here to torment, to coax
a truth from her closed mouth.
We ask only that she give herself over,
completely, to magic. As we have.

All her life she's clutched crayons, coloring
time any shade she prefers. Today
we're melting the crayons
to give her lightning. She can knit
tulip petals to keep them
from falling asleep when she talks to them,
which she often does. They answer
in a language only she understands.

We're old. My white beard holds
several countries. She doesn't accept
the branch I offer with an albino possum
that isn't real but could be. The square
room begins to shake, walls cracking
as magic swells through her every cell—
a single thought can break
the ceiling and call down the sky. *This,*

she says, *is my birthday. I am eighty.*
Red boats move through me, perfect
tiny sailors guiding them safely home.

Angry Masks

Painting by James Ensor

In the gym shower
two men itemize
people they hate:

the more they talk,
the angrier they grow,
one guy making

tighter and tighter
circles, the other's
head bobbing back
and forth.
As they soap up, bodies
shining through steam,
they grimace—water

soothes nothing:
they dry, dress,
drive off.

Les Belles de Nuit

Pen and Ink by Paul Delvaux

Ladies of the evening,
moonflower vines,
elastic white chalk,

or four o'clocks yawning
purple. Behind them
a chiseled mountain,

carved cracks scaring even
weeds away. Summer,
the rail car carrying

a killer turns into a
sunflower—he leaps off,
lands in a yellow petal clock,

clings to the second hand.
The ladies and each building
hear his screams. His grip goes—

falling,
his name hits dirt
before he does.

Venus Asleep

A skeleton and an
Edwardian lady meet
in Rome—she's

a red evening
primrose. His grin

keeps the rowdiest
seed quaking under
earth's stone hat.

Underwater Vision

Painting by Odilon Redon

Get far enough out, drop anchor
and leap into the lake. In the cabin,
your life consists of lists
and exhaust. Underwater, you return
to school with minnows, find mysteries

written on the underside of a lily pad,
a yellow flower
hoisted above a green rope. Ripples
and sun-bits slide toward the bottom.
Be careful—

boulders hide here, could split
your head open. New worlds offer risk.
To the loon, the risk floats mainly above
the water. She dives,
stays under for half a minute,

bobs up while danger looks away. You
swim fatigued back to the boat,
pull yourself over its edge, row
to half open cupboards, bananas
with brown spots.

Parade Amoureuse

Painting by Francis Picabia

Love, so outdated, I find it
only in resale shops
and lawn sales with
bent irons and obsolete
board games—it holds
a certain charm, like finding

a 1961 Montana map
in the glove compartment
and remembering sex
in a Butte motel, barn owls
barking in pines.

The Image as Produced by Automatic Writing

Photograph by Brassaï

We return to our roily city, sky
teasing us like red meat
before a fly, a ghost knitting
a white ruffled shirt
on top of a billboard
that says only
"John 3:16."

I told him: You're a big city girl now.

He told me: Am not.
Am a country boy who sits on a porch,
loving guns and YouTube.

We're in love. In hate.
Sinking,
thinking we're rising
over tree tops. Years

mount up
like unpaid traffic tickets.

Giraffe Mask

The Elephant of Celebes

Painting by Max Ernst

An elephant feeds a mirage
to a wooden floor.
The entire Industrial Revolution

fits into the black-shelled beast. Knock.
It feels nothing.
If you get eaten, relax

inside the belly. Headless,
a woman tries to speak the poem
she wrote about loss she told

to fish swimming overhead.
They swim away. An orange
remark, you crave a sunny walk

beyond a blue pergola. The elephant
remembers a savannah
and a graham-cracker brown river.

This is how it will be: you looking
for blue, the animal looking
for you looking for blue.

Dog, Come Here into the Dark House. Come Here, Black Dog.

Etching by Leonora Carrington

At night when barred owls
ask who cooks for you, she sits
by the window. No one

cooks for her. She has a black dog
and coral night. The moon
offers stepladders of gleam. Preferring the dark,

she closes shutters at dawn. Of course
people say she must be lonely. They're right.
She thinks loneliness is like a maple tree

she counts on to change colors. Besides,
with a black dog who could feel too alone?
His tail made of butterflies and

zinnias. He barks and a glass of red wine
appears. Quite the dog about town
yet faithful as a hard crossword puzzle

in the Sunday paper. Her windows open
and close but rarely break.
Cracking glass will announce

her own death. She sees it faintly
through dusty panes, smiles
before turning away.

Two Blue Horses by a Red Rock

Painting by Franz Marc

A horse imagines grass
and clover, pauses,
trots. Death comes quickly—

air out the nostrils,
ivory mist. Legs buckle,
soul slipping out
her left ear to a red rock—

she tests wind
for an exit, rises
toward sky's barn
At dawn
another horse comes, red
weathervane—morning,

a warm blanket, apples.

La Chasse au Lion

Prehistoric eyes on canvas:
stilted heads, stilted bodies.
Blunt green stashed

in a yellow field: a lion watches
her mate pounce on nervous eyes
of a gun—

it's as if the painting
wants to blow you away
just for looking at it.

Giraffe on Fire

This morning I couldn't shake
a dream about being back in grade school,
only it wasn't my school. A stranger,

grown up, I tried to fit myself
behind the desk, tried to hide in plain sight.
The teacher, a man made of step ladders
and spoons, knew I didn't belong, made me
swallow mud. I woke up, poured coffee. The paper

said a North Sea gas leak could be flammable
and hard to contain. Nature keeps spiking
a fever, the doctor playing golf.
A neighborhood giraffe walks by the picture
window, on fire, eating leaves from

our maple tree. On a sill our Meyer lemon
opens her yellow mouth and blurts something
that annoys the giraffe who takes his flaming
skin into the next yard. School buses start
sliding by, blue kids stuffed into seats,

oranges in a crate. They know their fate
is to be devoured. I haven't quite accepted
mine yet. I'm a sleepwalker, fully awake,
desiring sleep, dreamless sleep,
but not death, not that.

Lobster Telephone

Painting by Salvador Dalí

My day keeps ringing.
Hello, hello.
Nothing human responds,

ever. I've quit expecting
the how are you and the I'm fine.
I'm not fine. I'm talking to something
less than, more than, human.

Then again, it's just as hard to know
what people are really saying. Or
what I'm saying, for that matter. Words

fling out like paint hitting a wall,
a sorry blue spatter. Oh no,
more ringing. Last week I think
I wanted it to be a zebra,
black and white, a good runner. Today

it's a lobster, I'm sure of it,
claws click. We
have little to say. The sea,
like a stranger on a party line,
tries to horn in. Waves slide

into my living room. I float clear
across the world, never leave home.

The Call of the Night

Painting by Paul Delvaux

Vegetation instead of hair,
a woman holds

a lamp, walks on dry
bones, stands still,

knows each rock is
alive—something terrible

might happen.
Or not. The sky,

lighter near
the mountain,

a long walk,
lamp weak.

The Onlooker

Painting by Edith Rimmington

A large eyeball stares
from a shell, sees desires
to kill or be at peace,
to rape or create safety.

I often want to stick
a pin in it. What if it grew
a new eye? I could smash
the shell. It would
rebuild in my blood, swim
up to my heart and kill me.

What to do with an eye that
widens and never closes?

Give in. Hope
it is merciful.

Young Redon at Peyrelebade

As a child I sought
shadows: mice
scurrying under a chair
at dusk.

Our respectable floors,
ribs cracking
under my every step.
Shy and nervous, dreams
became poppies, smiling
spiders and masks.
I hid behind curtains,
saw the moon had human hair.
Always someone looked
for me. I learned how

to avoid the cellar
of family conversations.
Instead, I had pink trees,
smoke plumes. Dawn,
my favorite time: the sun
broke her copper bowl
on a stair. The moon crouched.

I have my own family now.
Ari's head on a pillow,
a boat drifting in lilies.
Stems catch on his breath.

Under his lids a dream slides
into place. He hides there
until morning. When he wakes
he smiles as if we have shared

the same room without recognizing
each other.

Aphrodisiac Jacket

Painting by Salvador Dalí

Changing to the Weather Station
from *I Love Lucy,* I see we aren't safe,
never were—I could stand outside
and bang a spoon against a pot,
tell the storm to vamoose. That never
even scares off groundhogs. Or

I could wear this jacket, liqueur glasses
painted on, and say: This is how
it will be forever, one surprise
after another rolling out
like conveyer-belt chocolates,
a talisman jacket to prevent

break-up. I won't say divorce.
We can't marry anyway. Even if
you adore the jacket, the hurricane
edges closer to the shore, closer
to our door. A small moment
in the eye. Stillness.
We've made it.

Rain beating on shingles—
a tree trunk's terrible crack.

Soft Construction with Boiled Beans (Premonition of a Civil War)

Painting by Salvador Dalí

The water boils away, a stench
and ruined pot. We set a nice table,
avoid the trombone anchorman
who plays too loud. You yearn
for a cleaner sky,
for a polish to shine
the sun a shiny gold button
on a cloud's open shirt. Someday

we'll have to bleach our bones
before presenting them to the Office
of Bone Collection.

As morning darkens we scream,
not with mouths, but with pores.
No one hears. Perhaps
we still look normal.

The Third of May

Painting by Goya

Blood on hills red
with poppies. When you try praying,
crows pluck up your words,
fly off. At night, mamelukes,
men with families back home,
crack guns over faces. Your arms
rise above your head. Flesh
must sink to bullet level. The shooters
don't stop—it's necessary

to make sure. Behind you,
a city doesn't shake or fall. Buildings
look as they did yesterday.
So much the same but smells

unbearable. Soldiers have
more work to do.

The Red City

Painting by Paul Delvaux

Are they people or ruins?
Do bones which long ago shed gender
care, held together
by light and promise? Quiet,

an androgyne walks by.
Sky, a death watching us,
azure as death is

azure. Sometimes. Nobody's
alarmed the meaning
of life hasn't yet been
put in a zoo.
Stand, walk, or recline—

it's all the same to
the skeleton who shops
at only the best Ideas.

Dream Caused by the Flight of a Bee around a Pomegranate a Second before Waking Up

Painting by Salvador Dalí

Tail high, a tiger leaps. Sometimes
a naked woman or man lounges
on the grass. Love,

last night I dreamed
in my old grade school you
viciously killed a piece of chalk.
A bee stung me. I began to talk
in a language I didn't know.

You ran off with the bee. I woke up
alone. The tiger beside me.

Fur Breakfast

Art Object by Méret Oppenheim

To gain the friendship of objects,
I beg the vacuum cleaner to swallow me whole.
I'm dangerous

around a cranberry red candy dish.
The furry cup and saucer shame me.
I become both coffee and sugar,

fingers touching the handle.
The cup stretches in a spot of sunlight,
ripples the sip.

Marcel Duchamp

> *"Duchamp is a cheat! Anyone can do what he does."*
> — L.L. McCleffrey

Arm in arm we're
            swaying oh
        Marcel you cad I saw
    you flirting with Paris
Hilton but I'll take my
        chances
                the last time
I saw happiness
            a urinal
        on a wall
                an ironing board
    with teeth and
the last time   I saw sadness
        nothing
            nothing
    but god   how good it looked
afraid of
                nothing
        everything

Plop
The string
Falls

        on canvas
            could be anyone

any string
any canvas

Plop   fall   Marcel you

    pick me
up place me on a shelf
            made of leeches
        Saltines

Three a.m. in the Art Gallery

Black peels off
the wall. A guard
sleeps while Monet
drowns in a color
pool. Dust
creeps onto a stone
Buddha, decorates
his knees. Streetlights
clog each room,
a tomb, alive,
until morning.

The Q Symphony

Painting by Leonora Carrington

Music lolls on the porch,
starts to pace. Tatekah and Qemliza
play instruments stored in a firefly's blink.

Notes swing party lights from the crabapple
to the clarkia. Listening slides
a pink cat tongue into an atom's

dark wedge. Tatekah feeds
three wolves treble clefs. Hungry,
they leave no bones. Qemliza

sews a gown made of onions,
push pins, and damask. She'll look her best
when the Symphony King slips out

from behind the garage door,
appears briefly, and returns to Silence—
songs sleep for millennia until

they're born on a blue night that stretches
from galaxy to galaxy,
thinner than an eye lash.

Landscape from a Dream

Painting by Paul Nash

The Dorset coast erodes,
primps while the sun marks
any prayer return to sender.
A polar bear cloud's jaws
can break the Arctic Circle.
Not hungry, she moves on.
Two rocks quarrel. One says,

"Love me!" His boyfriend
winks at a snail. 1942.
Bullets bleed between waves.

Listen hard,
    gulls again,
        flying off
            to the Secret
                they use to line nests.

Nocturnal Garden with Buildings

Painting by Gabriele Münter

A yellow hibiscus dumps blossoms. Nightfall,
purple tempera paint,
makes our neighborhood vanish. The moon
hangs onto Earth's leg like a three-year-old.

Buds strain to open, feel death
seize roots. Lightning aches
along roads turned to steam. Morning
shakes in leaves—they begin
to unfold.

Nude Ascending a Skycase

After Duchamp

My nude maple wants to leave
the ground. Winter holds its roots
tight, cold hands all day,

all night. I sip Chock Full O Nuts,
watch my maple walk up
a cloud stairway, a rare occurrence

here where things stay put,
learn to dissolve,
like hope or intelligence. So go,

dear tree, up, up and away.
Sway on heaven's boulevards.
Shade Bette Davis.

The Flying Ur Jar

Painting by Leonora Carrington

A motionless white horse,
a breathing handkerchief. Doors
define us more than they do you.

We easily enter and leave our spaces,
name them or set them on fire. I wouldn't
survive long among your locks and keys.

I don't own the horse. No one owns anything.
When the Ur Jar slides down the sky
like a shirt falling off a hanger, we

offer no prayers or possessions. It floats
and watching is a kind of prayer. Your people
use words to pray—do they bring

the Jar closer? Many here believe
the Jar will sprinkle us with death.
We'll gather what falls, breathe it in, eat.

We have no desire to die and
a great desire to die. We study the angle
of light as the Jar drifts over, listen

for ancient songs our ancestors sang
when they too floated overhead, songs
like a wind chime hung from a star.

Georgia O'Keefe's Flowers

All you can do is descend—
no returning. Your eyes
become petals, your bones stems.
Law is vanquished; no up, no out,
only falling. Under you, time is
red wind.

You think you're invisible,
only one more
contributing odor. You find
dead relatives—maybe this
is Atlantis or The Emerald City.

You cannot touch them: like you,
they go down, deeper
into a vortex. Your name slides
off you, an old jacket. You
dangle. The old life
built on a certainty of roofs
disappears. Buds enter each pore.
Nothing can stop you from opening.

Pastoral

Painting by Leonora Carrington

You hover above a thin white blanket.
Wind

bends the birch nearby
yet it stands—you envy it. You
can hardly tell human
from animal, your owl eyes,
a hand like a fox paw. You want
the world to still, to stop
its endless turning—

that means your death,
everyone's death. You say let it spin,
which it does, as if trying to weave
a lethal wonderful calm.

Acknowledgments

I would like extend special thanks to art historian Dr. Ilene Lieberman, and appreciation to the editors of the following magazines for publishing work from this collection.

"Angry Masks" | *Double Entendre*

"Aphrodisiac Jacket" | *Big Pulp*

"Belles de Nuit" | *Adirondack Review*

"The Call of the Night" | *Ixion* (England)

"La Chasse Au Lion" | *Great Lakes Review*

"Composition with Glove" | *Contemporary World Literature*

"The Dance on the Shore" | *Nit & Wit Review*

"Daybreak" | *The Original Van Gogh's Ear Anthology*

"Dick and Betsy Smith" | *Caught in the Net* (England)

"Dog, Come Here…." | *Philadelphia Stories*

"Dream Caused By…" | *Empty Mirror*

"The Elephant of the Celebes" | *Painters And Poets*

"Empire of Lights" | *South Townsville Micro Poetry Journal* (Australia)

"Epona, Goddess of the Herds" | *Ekphrastic*

"Euclid's Last Stand" | *Eclectica*

"The Flying Ur Jar" | *Istanbul Literary Review*

"Franz Mark Painting Before The War" | *Mid-American Review*

"Fur Breakfast" | *Eclectica*

"Georgia O'Keefe's Flowers" | *The Cape Rock, Greatest Hits* (chapbook), Pudding House Press

"The Giantess" | *Moonshot*

"Giraffe on Fire" | *Weber: The Contemporary West*

"The Greeting" | *Rain Dog* (England)

"The Hopes at Home" | *Drexel Online Journal*

"The Image as Produced by Automatic Writing" | *Weber: The Contemporary West*

"In Chrustov's House Near St. Prex" | *Ekphrastia Gone Wild* (anthology), Ain't Got No Press

"Kurt Schwitters" | *Istanbul Literary Review*

"Landscape from a Dream" | *Ixion* (England)

"Lobster Telephone" | *Spinozablue*

"Loplop Introduces Loplop" | *Lost Coast Review*

"Loplop Introduces a Young Girl" | *Rhino*

"Loplop Presents a Flower" | *Big Pulp*

"Loplop" | *Weber: The Contemporary West*

"Marcel Duchamp" | *Windsor Review* (Canada)

"Marionette Theatre" | *Bookends Review*

"Mystery and Melancholy of a Street" | *Weber: The Contemporary West*

"Nocturnal Garden With Buildings" | *Minetta Review*

"Nude Ascending a Skycase" | *Poetrystory*

"Odilon Redon's World" | *Owen Wister Review*

"The Onlooker" | *A New Ulster* (Northern Ireland)

"Parade Amoureuse" | *The Part-Time Postmodernist*

"The Q Symphony" | *The Leopard Seal*

"The Red City" | *Cider Press Review*

"Rendezvous of the Friends" | *Spinozablue*

"The Return of Ulysses" | *Loch Raven Review*

"Soft Construction" | *Empty Mirror*

"El Sueno" | *Minetta Review*

"Syssigy" | *Fat City Review*

"The Third of May" | *Amsterdam Quarterly* (The Netherlands)

"Three a.m. in the Art Gallery" | *Cyclo-Flame*

"Triumphal Entry" | *Double Entendre*

"Two Blue Horses by a Red Rock" | *Edgar*
"Underwater Vision" | *Two Words For All*
"Van Gogh's Crows" | *Rusty Truck / Contralto Crows*
(chapbook), Green Fuse Press
"Venus Asleep" | *Samsara*
"Vincent Van Gogh" | *Indiana Review / Evergreen* (chapbook),
Bragdon Press
"Waiting for Grace and Betty, 19874" | *Black Moon*
"Young Redon at Peyrelebade" | *Outerbridge / Cicadas in the
Apple Tree* (chapbook), Palanquin Press

About Kenneth Pobo

Kenneth Pobo's work has appeared in *Hawaii Review, The Fiddlehead, Mudfish, Indiana Review, Madison Review, Caesura, Eclectica* and more. He is author of over twenty poetry collections and chapbooks, including his collection *Bend of Quiet,* which won the 2014 Blue Light Press Book Award. He teaches creative writing at Widener University in Pennsylvania.

www.ingramcontent.com/pod-product-compliance
Lightning Source LLC
Chambersburg PA
CBHW022115050726
47591CB00002B/798